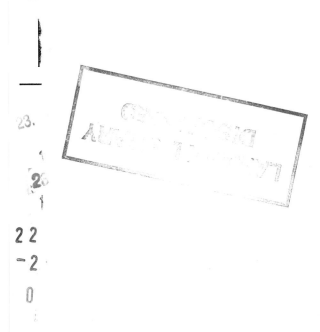

Celebrate!

United States

Robyn Hardyman

FRANKLIN WATTS
LONDON•SYDNEY

This edition first published in 2009
by Franklin Watts

Franklin Watts
338 Euston Road
London NW1 3BH

Franklin Watts Australia
Level 17/207 Kent Street
Sydney, NSW 2000

A CIP catalogue record for this book is available from the British Library.
Dewey no: 917.3

ISBN 978 0 7496 8423 5

Printed in China

Franklin Watts is a division of Hachette Children's Books, an Hachette UK company.
www.hachette.co.uk

Note to parents and teachers concerning websites:
In the book every effort has been made by the Publishers to ensure that websites are suitable for children, that they are of the highest educational value, and that they contain no inappropriate or offensive material. However, because of the nature of the Internet, it is impossible to guarantee that the contents of these sites will not be altered. We advise that Internet access is supervised by a responsible adult.

For The Brown Reference Group Ltd
Project Editor: Sarah Eason
Designer: Paul Myerscough
Picture Researcher: Maria Joannou
Indexer: Claire Throp
Design Manager: David Poole
Managing Editor: Miranda Smith
Editorial Director: Lindsey Lowe

Consultant Editor
Peter Lewis
Writer and Editor for the American Geographical Society, New York

Author
Robyn Hardyman

Contents

Welcome to the United States 4

History Highlights 6

Fly the Flag 10

Hymn to the United States 12

Regions of the United States 14

What's Cooking? 16

How Do I Say...? 18

Stories and Legends 20

Art and Culture 22

Make Your Own
Dream Catcher 24

Sports and Leisure 26

Festivals and Holidays 28

Glossary 30

Find Out More 31

Index 32

Welcome to the United States

The United States is the world's most powerful country. It forms a large part of the continent of North America, and includes a huge variety of landscapes. A good number of the people of the United States originally came from many different countries. Parts of the culture, such as films and music, are popular all over the world.

The United States is a **federal republic**. It has fifty **states** and one federal area, the District of Columbia. The capital city of Washington, D.C. is there. The country is governed by a **president** and **Congress**. Congress is made up of two bodies: the **Senate**, which has two elected senators (representatives) from each state, and the House of Representatives. Congress makes laws. The third branch of government is the Supreme Court.

National emblem

The **emblem** of the United States is the bald eagle. It appears on the back of coins and on the Great Seal (left). The eagle represents freedom and became the country's national emblem in 1782.

A big country

Forty-eight of the American states are grouped together. Alaska, the biggest state, is separated from the others by Canada. The island state of Hawaii is about 3,840 kilometres west of California in the Pacific Ocean. The United States is so big that there is a time difference of six hours between Hawaii in the west and Maine on the east coast. The United States also possesses five major **territories**: Puerto Rico and the United States Virgin Islands in the Caribbean, and American Samoa, Guam and the Northern Mariana Islands in the Pacific.

AMERICAN FACTS

FULL NAME	United States of America
CAPITAL CITY	Washington, D.C.
AREA	9.8 million square km
POPULATION IN 2008	305 million
MAIN LANGUAGE	English
MAIN RELIGION	Christianity
CURRENCY	U.S. dollar

Statue of Liberty

The Statue of Liberty stands at the entrance to New York Harbor. It is a powerful symbol of the United States that is recognized all over the world. The statue was given to the American people by France in 1886. Her torch represents freedom, and the book she carries represents the law.

History Highlights

People have been living in the land that makes up the United States for thousands of years. However, the country did not become a single nation until 1776.

The first people to inhabit North America came from Asia. They travelled there using a **land bridge**, more than 12,000 years ago. Native Americans are descended from these people. They lived by fishing along the coasts. In the cold north they hunted for food. In the warmer south they began to farm, growing crops such as maize and beans. Each tribe had its own language, religion and customs. One of the biggest tribes was the Sioux. Other tribes included the Cree, the Apache and the Navajo.

Arrival of Europeans

The first European explorers reached North America perhaps as early as the eleventh century. In 1585, an early English settler named John White made a series of paintings of the local Algonquin people (left). Some Native Americans helped the Europeans to settle. Others moved to the area known as the 'Great Plains' to keep their traditional way of life.

Totem poles

Totem poles are sculptures carved by the native tribes along the Pacific northwest coast of the United States. They are wonderful works of art, decorated with symbols to represent a family's history, beliefs and experiences.

European settlers

Most early **immigrants** to North America came from England and Spain. The Spanish settled in the south. The English made their first permanent settlement at Jamestown, Virginia, in 1607. Many early immigrants were **Puritans**. They went to the United States to escape religious **persecution** in their home countries. By 1634, New England, for example, had been settled by some 10,000 Puritans. By 1733, Britain ruled thirteen **colonies** along the east coast of North America. The people were ruled by the British, and had to pay taxes to them.

Independence

People in the colonies became unhappy about paying taxes to England. They also did not want to be ruled by a king who lived so far away. The thirteen colonies united and fought for independence in the American Revolution (1775–83). They won on 3rd September 1783. The painting (right) shows the 1776 signing of the Declaration of Independence.

DID YOU KNOW?
In 1620 the Pilgrim Fathers arrived in the United States aboard the *Mayflower*.

American Civil War

In the eighteenth century, European settlers moved into the southern states of Louisiana, Florida and Texas, as well as Hawaii. They set up farms called plantations, **and** slaves were shipped from West Africa to work on them. Not everyone agreed with slavery, and in 1861 the southern states fought the northern states over their right to own slaves. The American Civil War lasted until 1865. The southern states lost, and slavery was made illegal.

Abraham Lincoln

Abraham Lincoln (1809–65, left) was president of the United States from 1861 to 1865. He was one of the leaders of the anti-slavery movement. He was assassinated in 1865 by a supporter of the southern states.

Prosperity and power

By 1914, the United States was the richest country in the world. Its factories made cars and many other goods. The boom ended suddenly in 1929 with a **depression**. After World War II (1939–45), the economy managed to recover. The United States became the most powerful nation in the world.

Martin Luther King Jnr

Martin Luther King Jnr (1929–68, right) was the leader of the American civil rights movement. He campaigned for equal rights for African Americans in the United States. King urged his supporters to use non-violent protest to change the laws that allowed black people to be treated as inferior citizens. He was shot and killed in 1968.

World superpower

Since the Soviet Union's collapse in the late 1980s, the United States has been the world's main superpower. Its wealth and influence are felt everywhere. In 1969, American astronauts landed on the Moon, and since then America's influence and culture have spread across the globe. Today, people worldwide use American computers, listen to American music and watch American films. American food chains can be seen all over the world, and the U.S. military is at work in many countries. There are few places that have not been influenced by the United States in one way or another.

Fly the Flag

The American flag is made up of thirteen red and white horizontal stripes, and a blue rectangle of fifty white stars. The stripes represent the thirteen original colonies, and the stars represent the states. The flag is commonly known as the 'Stars and Stripes'. The colonies first adopted it as their flag on 14th June 1777. Today, Americans celebrate Flag Day on 14th June every year.

Southern flag

This was the first flag of the southern states, who fought in the Civil War in 1861–65 (see page 8). It was known as the 'Stars and Bars'.

DID YOU KNOW?
The colours of the flag are intended to symbolize the qualities of the American people. White stands for peace, red for bravery and strength, and blue for truth, loyalty and justice.

Well travelled

The flag is generally flown on public buildings. Some people fly it from their homes. It has even been flown on the Moon! In 1969, American astronaut Buzz Aldrin planted it on the Moon's surface during the *Apollo 11* mission, when men landed on the Moon for the very first time.

Try this!

Make a top hat for Flag Day

- *Cut out a rectangle of white cardboard, measuring 22.5 cm by 60 cm.*

- *Cut out two strips of red paper, measuring 5 cm by 60 cm.*

- *Cut out one strip of blue paper, measuring 2.5 cm by 60 cm.*

- *Use glue to stick one red strip of paper along the top edge of the white cardboard. Stick the blue strip along the bottom edge. Then glue the other red strip of paper along the middle of the remaining white area.*

- *Cut out some white stars from paper, and glue them all along the blue stripe.*

- *Roll up the rectangle to make a top hat that fits your head. Then glue the ends together securely.*

5 cm

5 cm

60 cm

22.5 cm

Hymn to the United States

The 'Star-Spangled Banner' is the national anthem of the United States. Its words describe the country's flag.

The words of the national anthem come from a poem written by Francis Scott Key (pictured below). He wrote the poem in 1814, to mark the American victory in a battle against the British at Fort McHenry, Maryland. The **patriotic** words were set to a popular tune, which became a well-known song. It was officially recognized in 1916 by the President and became the anthem on 3rd March 1931.

DID YOU KNOW?
During the eighteenth and nineteenth centuries, a song called *Hail Columbia* was often sung as the United States' national anthem. The music was composed in 1789 to be played at the inauguration of George Washington.

WEB LINKS ▼▼▼▼▼▼▼▼▼
To hear the U.S. national anthem go to:
www.national-anthems.net/US

The music

The tune of the 'Star-Spangled Banner' existed before the lyrics. It belonged to a popular drinking song that was written by Englishman John Stafford Smith in the 1760s.

National pride

Baseball players stand while the national anthem is sung before a Major League Baseball All-Star Game in San Francisco, California.

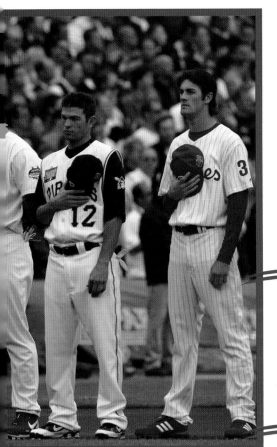

Moving words

Although Francis Scott Key's poem has four verses, only the first one (shown right) is usually sung. The fourth is sometimes added on **formal** occasions. It has a reputation for being difficult to sing.

'O! say can you see, by the dawn's early light,
What so proudly we hailed at the twilight's last gleaming.
Whose broad stripes and bright stars through the perilous fight,
O'er the ramparts we watched were so gallantly streaming.
And the rockets' red glare, the bombs bursting in air,
Gave proof through the night that our flag was still there.
Oh, say does that star-spangled banner yet wave
O'er the land of the free and the home of the brave?'

Regions of the United States

The United States stretches from the Arctic Circle in the north, to the Caribbean Sea in the south. This means that the country's climate and landscape vary greatly from one region to another.

Two large mountain ranges tower over the western United States: the Sierra Nevada and the Rocky Mountains. The Rocky Mountains run from north to south like a giant backbone. To the east of the Sierra Nevada, the River Colorado has cut through the high land to form the stunning Grand Canyon (right).

Rivers and lakes

The United States has many important rivers, including the Missouri, Mississippi, Ohio, Rio Grande and Colorado. The Great Lakes, which include Lake Superior (shown left), are a chain of freshwater lakes that form part of the **border** with Canada. They are the largest group of freshwater lakes on Earth.

National parks

There are fifty-eight official national parks in the United States. They include magnificent scenery and geographical features, such as the geysers in Yellowstone National Park (shown right). The parks are sometimes referred to as the United States' 'crown jewels'.

WEB LINKS

Find out more about America's national parks at: www.nps.gov

Climate

Almost all parts of the country have warm or hot summers. In the west, the mountains and deserts are very dry. In Death Valley in the Mojave Desert, California, temperatures reach 50°C. In the southeast, it is warm and wet for much of the year. Further north and east it is cooler and drier.

AMERICAN FACTS

LONGEST RIVERS	Missouri 3,767 km, Mississippi 3,734 km, Rio Grande 3,034 km
HIGHEST MOUNTAIN	Mount McKinley, Alaska 6,194 m
LARGEST CITIES	New York City, Los Angeles, Chicago

Natural disasters

The west coast of the United States suffers from earthquakes. The city of San Francisco was badly hit in 1906, and again in 1989. In 1980, Mount St Helens in Washington erupted violently, causing enormous damage and loss of life. Mount Rainier (below) is another active volcano in Washington state.

What's Cooking?

American cooking is as varied as its population. The wonderful variety of food includes great recipes and dishes from all over the world.

The style of cooking in each region of the United States has been influenced by the people who have settled there, and the ingredients available locally. In the northeast coastal states they make wonderful seafood dishes, such as clam chowder. In the south, dishes include barbecued pork ribs and corn bread. In the southwest, near Mexico, they use lots of chilli and spices. In California, the Asian population has brought dishes from their countries of origin to homes and restaurants.

Fast food

Fast food is available all over the country, in many different kinds of food shops. Burgers, fried chicken and hot dogs can be bought on almost any city street. Chinese egg rolls, Mexican *tacos* and Japanese *sushi* are also popular.

WEB LINKS

Find many more Creole and Cajun recipes at: www.louisianafoods.com/recipes/

Eating out

Americans love barbecues. Southerners particularly like barbecued pork. Independence Day on 4th July is a popular day for picnics throughout the country.

New Orleans

New Orleans is a city at the mouth of the River Mississippi. Spanish and French colonists settled there first. In the nineteenth century, they were joined by many freed African slaves. The result has been a unique and fine cuisine, known as Creole and Cajun cooking. The dish on the left is called Creole Shrimp Gumbo.

What's on the menu?

This menu is typical of a meal served in New Orleans.

Creole Gumbo
Richly flavoured soup with chicken, spicy sausage and seafood

Creole Jambalaya
Rice with chicken, sausages, tomatoes and spices

Oysters Rockefeller
Oysters with green herbs

Banana Foster
Dessert made from bananas and vanilla ice cream

Try this!

Let's make a hamburger

Ingredients:
100 g beef burger
1 large tomato
2 dill pickles
soft white bread roll topped with sesame seeds
mayonnaise
tomato ketchup
few lettuce leaves

You will need to ask an adult to help you with the cooking and cutting for this recipe. Heat a griddle pan, or frying pan, over a medium heat. When it is hot, put the burger in the pan. Brown it on both sides for 5 minutes. Slice the tomato thickly, and the pickles thinly. Carefully cut the roll in half lengthwise. Spread some mayonnaise and/or ketchup on the bottom half, and then put some lettuce leaves and a slice of tomato on it. Lay the cooked burger on top of the tomato, and add the sliced pickles, tomato and more ketchup or mayonnaise to suit your taste. Finally, put the other half of the roll on top. Enjoy!

How Do I Say...?

The population of the United States is made up of people from all over the world. As a result, hundreds of languages are spoken there.

English is the official language in the United States. Most citizens speak English, but on any street you are likely to hear many different languages. In the big cities, people who **originate** from one country often live in the same area. This means that their native language is kept alive. Spanish is very widely spoken, especially in the southern states, because millions of **Hispanic** people, from Central and South America, live there.

DID YOU KNOW?
Over 300 languages are spoken in the United States.

Chinatown

The United States has the largest population of Chinese outside of China. In the cities, many Chinese people live in an area called Chinatown. In the United States, the biggest Chinatown is in San Francisco (shown left). Here people speak Mandarin and Cantonese Chinese.

Some American sayings

'By the yard, life is hard. By the inch, it's a cinch.'
'If you can't stand the heat, get out of the kitchen.'
'Good fences make good neighbours.'
'Never miss a good chance to shut up.'
'A stitch in time saves nine.'

Native American languages

Before the Europeans arrived, Native Americans spoke many different languages. Many of these died out along with the natives' traditional ways of life, when the settlers took their lands. Some languages survived, and are still spoken today. In Oregon and Washington, the Chinook people speak Chinookan. The Algonquin languages are spoken from the Rocky Mountains to New England, while the Wintuan languages are spoken in California. Pictured left is a member of the Pawnee tribe in traditional dress.

Webster's

Noah Webster wrote the first large American English dictionary, *An American Dictionary of the English language*, in 1828.

Stories and Legends

The United States has many legendary characters and traditional tales. But not all the stories are made up. Its history is so colourful and exciting that the adventures of real people have become legends.

Paul Bunyan is one of the greatest characters in American folklore. He is a giant lumberjack who is brave and fearless. He and his faithful blue ox, Babe, have great adventures and perform miraculous tasks. He leaps over mountains, and digs lakes as drinking holes. He was made popular by journalist James MacGillivray, who began writing about him in 1906. Bunyan quickly became a folk hero. Statues of Bunyan and Babe are found in the northern United States.

Brer Rabbit

Brer Rabbit is an African-American folk hero. He is a trickster, who constantly outwits Brer Fox. Tales about him were taken to the United States by African slaves.

Old Man Winter

Native Americans have a story to explain the changing seasons. Old Man Winter lives in the frozen north, while Summer Queen lives in the warm south. Once a year, Old Man Winter walks south, bringing snow and ice. After six months, Summer Queen forces him to return to his cold home, and she brings the spring.

Davy Crockett

Davy Crockett (1786–1836, right) was a real person, whose extraordinary life made him a legend in his own lifetime. He is often called 'the king of the wild frontier'. He ran away from home as a boy, and lived a life full of adventure, fighting and hunting in the western United States. He was an amazing hunter, said to have once killed 150 bears in six months. He was also a politician. He fought with the Texans in their struggle for independence from Mexico, and died a hero at the Battle of the Alamo.

WEB LINKS ▼▼▼▼▼▼▼▼▼▼▼▼▼
Find out lots more about American folk tales at: www.americanfolklore.net/

DID YOU KNOW?
Some pretty tough outlaws have become legends in the United States. These include Billy the Kid and Jesse James.

HUCKLEBERRY FINN.

Mark Twain

Mark Twain was the name under which Samuel Langhorne Clemens (1835–1910) published his books. He was one of the best-known writers of his time, and has been called 'the father of American literature'. His most famous novels were *The Adventures of Tom Sawyer* (1876) and *The Adventures of Huckleberry Finn* (1884, left).

Art and Culture

Many aspects of American popular culture have spread across the world. Wherever you go, people listen to American music, watch American films and television programmes, and wear American-style clothes. But there is more to American culture than television soaps and pop music.

The American film industry makes the most popular and most profitable films in the world. Many of the big blockbusters are made by a few major studios based in Hollywood, California. American actors and actresses are famous worldwide.

Art

In the twentieth century, New York was an important centre of modern art. Artists such as Jackson Pollock (1912–56), Mark Rothko (1903–70), Andy Warhol (1928–1987) and Roy Lichtenstein (1923–97) worked and became famous there.

DID YOU KNOW?
Andy Warhol's work included pictures of cans of soup, and images of Marilyn Monroe.

Elvis Presley

Elvis Presley (1935–77) was the 'King of Rock 'n' Roll', or simply 'The King'. He was the most popular singer in the world during the 1950s and 1960s. He still remains popular today. In his lifetime he sold about 500 million records worldwide, with hits such as *Hound Dog*, *Blue Suede Shoes* and *It's Now Or Never*.

Architecture

The United States is full of great buildings, from Native American long houses to nineteenth-century mansions. One of its most famous architectural innovations is the skyscraper. When New York's towering Chrysler Building (left) was built in 1930 it was the tallest building in the world. It kept its world record just one year, until the Empire State Building was completed in 1931.

Music

The United States is the home of many kinds of music. The musical traditions of African-American slaves influenced the development of jazz, blues and soul music. These, in turn, influenced pop and rock. Some of the world's greatest American music stars are Louis Armstrong (jazz), James Brown (soul), Johnny Cash (country), Bob Dylan (folk), Jimi Hendrix (rock), Prince and Madonna (pop).

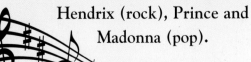

Make Your Own Dream Catcher

Native American dream catchers are round, to represent the Universe. Bad dreams are caught in the web, while good dreams pass through.

1 Put a small amount of glue on the ring and press down one end of the ribbon. Wind the ribbon tightly around the ring, until it is completely covered.

2 To make the web, loop the gold thread around the ring, as shown below.

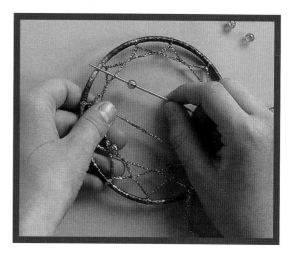

3 Use the needle to push more thread through the loops you have already made, as shown, and pull it tight. Continue until you have a second layer of loops.

4 Thread a bead on to every other loop. Make one more layer of loops, and tie the end of the thread neatly to the web, as shown above.

Dream catchers

Native Americans decorate their dream catchers with personal and sacred items, such as feathers and beads.

5 Tie a large bead to a length of gold thread, and tie it to the middle of the dream catcher.

6 To make a tail, tie the feather on to a length of thread. Push beads on to the thread, and tie it to the bottom of the ring as shown above.

DID YOU KNOW?
A dream catcher should be hung above your bed, so that the good dreams pass through the net and slide down the tail as you sleep.

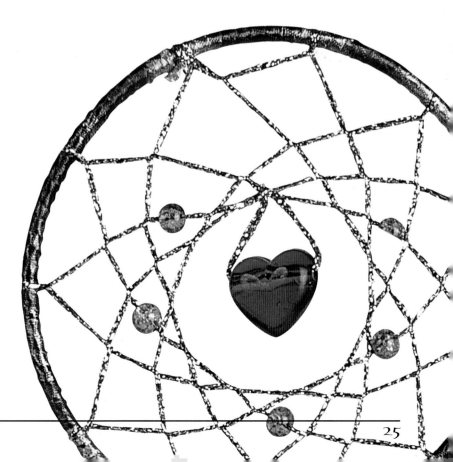

Sports and Leisure

The United States is so large that just about every leisure activity is enjoyed there. Basketball, baseball, ice hockey and American football are the major sports.

Playing sports is an important part of life at American schools and colleges. Four sports are particularly popular in the United States: baseball, basketball, ice hockey and football. Each of these has a major league, and millions of people follow their games. Baseball is the national sport. American football is the favourite game in the autumn.

Michael Jordan

Michael Jordan (born 1963, below) has been called the greatest basketball player of all time. He won the national basketball competition six times, and two Olympic gold medals. His worldwide fame helped to make basketball a popular sport in many other countries.

Golf and tennis

Golf is a very popular activity in the United States. Some of the best golfers in the world, such as Tiger Woods, are Americans. Tennis is popular, too. The country has produced some of the best tennis players of all time, including Pete Sampras, and Venus and Serena Williams.

Super Bowl Sunday

The National Football League's championship game is called the Super Bowl. Over the years it has become the most watched U.S. television broadcast of the year. It has almost become a national holiday. Friends and family get together to watch the game, eat, drink and enjoy themselves.

Thrill seekers

Americans love amusement parks! The Cedar Point Amusement Park in Sandusky, Ohio has seventeen roller coasters. That's more than any other park in the world!

The great outdoors

Americans go hiking in the hills, biking and skiing in the mountains and camping wherever there is a great view! The country has two long coastlines on the Atlantic and Pacific Oceans. Sports such as surfing and volleyball are favourite beach activities, particularly along California's coastline.

Festivals and Holidays

The people of the United States love celebrations. Some national holidays are important religious festivals, while others mark important events in the country's history.

Independence Day is on 4th July. This important national holiday celebrates the Declaration of Independence made by thirteen British colonies in 1776. People line the streets to watch parades, and celebrate with friends and family. As night falls, everyone gathers to watch spectacular firework displays.

Local colour

Thousands of local festivals take place in the United States. Some are tiny, while others are huge. In January, St Paul, Minnesota, hosts the largest winter carnival in the country. People watch parades and admire ice palaces and snow sculptures. Rodeos are popular in the west. At these, cowboys and cowgirls compete to stay on a bucking bronco, and lasso calves.

Thanksgiving

Thanksgiving is a huge national holiday. It is held on the last Thursday in November. It is to remember the time when early English settlers invited their Native American neighbours to a meal celebrating the first successful harvest in order to thank them for their help. The settlers served roast turkey, which is still the traditional Thanksgiving dish. President Abraham Lincoln first proclaimed a national Thanksgiving day in 1863.

Mardi Gras

Mardi Gras is an important, month-long celebration in the city of New Orleans. People dress in unusual colourful costumes and parade on floats through the streets.

Pow wows

Native Americans hold festivals called pow wows to celebrate their culture. Tribes gather together, dress in traditional costumes and perform their ancient dances (shown right). There may also be horse races and drumming contests. Pow wows can last many days.

Glossary

border frontier between countries

bucking bronco a wild horse that is difficult to tame

colonies territories ruled by non-natives

Congress the main legislative body of the United States

depression period of very severe economic slowdown, when businesses make less profit and many people lose their jobs

emblem symbol

federal republic system in which a group of states are ruled by a central government with an elected leader; each state has responsibility for local affairs

formal highly organized, not relaxed

Hispanic Spanish-speaking person from Central or South America

illegal against the law

immigrants people who move to another country to live there permanently

inauguration a ceremony at which a person is formally sworn in to their role

independence freedom from control by another country

land bridge strip of land between continents, often submerged under the sea

originate come from in the first place

patriotic inspired by love of a country, its flag, and its people

persecution severe mistreatment based on race, religion or political opinion

Pilgrim Fathers early settlers of the Plymouth Colony, which is in present-day Plymouth, Massachusetts

plantations large, working farms, usually in the southern states

president leader of a country, usually elected by the people

Puritans a group of people who were unhappy with the Church of England and wanted to 'purify' the church

revolution violent uprising by the people to overthrow the government

rodeos displays of cowboy skills in riding and controlling horses and other animals

Senate the upper house of the Congress

slaves people owned by other people

states geographical areas that make up a country such as the United States

sushi dish made with raw fish, rice and vegetables

tacos dish made with filled maize pancakes called *tortillas*

territories land owned and controlled by a country

Find Out More

Books

Brook, Henry. *The Wild West*
  Usborne
  ISBN: 978 0 7460 9374 0

Clements, Gillian. *A Picture History of
  Great Buildings.*
  Frances Lincoln
  ISBN: 978 1 8450 7488 3

Hamilton Murdoch, D. *DK Eyewitness
  North American Indian*
  Dorling Kindersley
  ISBN: 978 0 7566 1081 4

Pohl, Kathleen. *Looking at Countries:The
  USA.* Franklin Watts
  ISBN: 978 0 7496 8251 4

Twain, Mark. *Huckleberry Finn*
  Puffin Classics
  ISBN: 978 0 1413 2109 7

Websites

www.usatourist.com/index.html
This website has useful information on the
  country's states, cities and national parks.

www.nps.gov
The official website of the National Parks
  Service has everything about the
  country's spectacular national parks.

www.nativeamericans.com
This wonderful website is packed
  with information on all aspects of
  Native American life, from their
  history, languages and culture to
  their lives today.

http://americanhistory.about.com
This is a good place to find accessible
  information on American history.

http://americanart.si.edu/index3.cfm
The Smithsonian Museum is America's first
  federal art collection, dedicated to the
  enjoyment and understanding of
  American art, and its website is
  easy to use and informative.

Index

Alaska 5, 15
Aldrin, Buzz 11
Algonquin 6, 19
American Civil War 8, 10
American Revolution 7
Apache 6

baseball 13, 26
Battle of the Alamo 21
Brer Rabbit 20
Bunyan, Paul 20

California 5, 13, 15, 16,
    19, 22, 27
Canada 5, 14
Cree 6
Crockett, Davy 21

Death Valley 15
Declaration of
    Independence 7, 28

Flag Day 10, 11
Florida 8
football 26, 27

Grand Canyon 14
Great Lakes 14

Hawaii 5, 8

Independence Day 16, 28

Jamestown 7
Jordan, Michael 26

Key, Francis Scott 12, 13
King, Martin Luther, Jr. 9

Lake Superior 14
Lincoln, Abraham 8, 29
Louisiana 8

Maine 5
Mardi Gras 29
Mayflower 7
mountains 14, 15, 19, 27

Navajo 6
New England 7, 19
New Orleans 17, 29
New York 5, 15, 22, 23

Pawnee 19
pow wows 29
Pilgrim Fathers 7
Presley, Elvis 23

Puerto Rico 5
Puritans 7

rivers 14, 15, 17

San Francisco 13, 15, 18
Sierra Nevada 14
Sioux 6
skyscrapers 23
slaves 8, 17, 20, 23
'Star-Spangled Banner,
    The' 12, 13
Statue of Liberty 5
Super Bowl 27

tacos 16
Texas 8, 21
Thanksgiving 29
totem poles 7
Twain, Mark 21

Warhol, Andy 22
Washington, D.C. 4, 5
Washington, George 12
World War II 8

Yellowstone National
    Park 15